SOMETHING NEW
TO LEARN ABOUT
Lace

ARNALL-CULLIFORD KNITWEAR

SOMETHING NEW TO LEARN ABOUT **LACE**

Contents

Introduction

JEN ARNALL-CULLIFORD

As a beginner there were a few projects that felt like milestones in my development as a knitter – my first cable, my first pair of socks and my first lace scarf. The feeling of accomplishment I got as I completed those projects was extraordinary. I felt as if I was graduating from being just a knitter to being A Knitter. My first lace scarf wasn't even that complicated, it was a feather and fan pattern knitted in some lovely alpaca DK in moss green (I do love a good green!), but it was instantly obvious to me that lace holds so much possibility. In fact my next project was the Swallowtail Shawl by Evelyn A. Clark and my Ravelry notes say, *"This is just amazing. I can barely bear to put it down! I simply can't believe that I made an object of such beauty. It seems impossible!"*

That feeling of success reappears from time to time in my knitting to this day, and it is finishing a piece of lace that I still find most satisfying. Lace has its own rhythm on my needles, and I absolutely love how the stitches flow from one to another, creating organic shapes and a light, airy fabric. However, you don't have to spend long with knitters to realise that not everyone finds lace as intuitive as I do. Reading the pattern of yarn overs and decreases isn't straightforward, and without some help, it can be very frustrating to make a mistake and be unable to correct it. This volume aims to grow your confidence, helping you to avoid mistakes in the first place, giving you clear instructions on how to read your knitting, as well as some tutorials on fixing the inevitable mistakes that we all occasionally make.

There are also tutorials on blocking lace (the most magical process in all knitting!), as well as instructions on following lace charts and a special cast-on method for triangular lace shawls. Accompanying the stepwise tutorials are three beautiful lace designs that will allow you to try out your new skills; Donna Smith's Aphaca scarf and blanket are perfect for practising reading lace charts, Martina Behm's Nissolia shawl has clean lines in the leaf-lace edging which will help you to read your knitting and quickly fix any errors, and my Bithynica shawl features a garter tab cast on and larger lace holes that are made with double yarn overs.

Whichever project you choose, I hope that you will get that feeling of achievement as you work on your lace.

Chapter One

TUTORIALS:
BASIC LACE TECHNIQUES

PROJECT

DESIGNED BY **Donna Smith**

BASIC LACE TECHNIQUES

WHAT IS LACE?

Ranging from heirloom cobweb Shetland shawls, worked with patterning on every row, through to chunky accessories with a simple eyelet motif, the term lace covers an extraordinary variety of knitting patterns, each characterised by the presence of stable holes in the fabric. These holes are usually created by passing the yarn over the needle to increase a stitch and, unless increases are desired, each yarn over will be accompanied by a decrease, so that the stitch count remains constant.

The first part of this chapter will deal with creating yarn over holes in your knitting in a range of different situations, followed by how to read lace charts. With these basic skills you can dive in and try the beautiful Aphaca scarf or blanket by Donna Smith, which is the project at the end of the chapter.

WORKING YARN OVERS

A yarn over is a way of creating a new (or false) stitch in your knitting. Unlike other increases, the yarn over results in a purposeful hole in your knitting and is the basis of most lace patterns. How you form your yarn over depends on which stitches are worked either side of the increase. The following tutorials will walk you through the different possible situations.

WORKING A YARN OVER BETWEEN TWO KNIT STITCHES

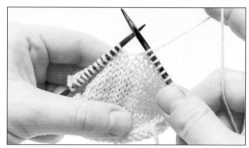

1 Work in pattern until you reach the first yarn over instruction. Your yarn will be at the rear of your work.

2 Bring the yarn to the front of your work between the needle tips.

3 Bring the yarn over the right needle tip, so that it returns to the rear of your work, and knit the next stitch as required.

4 When you work the following row (whether it is in the round or flat) you will see that the yarn over sits more diagonally across the needles than the surrounding stitches.

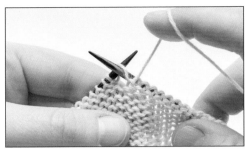 

5 Knit or purl into the yarn over as required by your pattern. Here the yarn over is being purled.

6 Having worked further up your pattern you will see that a hole has been made where you worked the yarn over.

WORKING A YARN OVER BETWEEN TWO PURL STITCHES

1 Work in pattern until you reach the first yarn over instruction. Your yarn will be at the front of your work.

2 Bring the yarn over the right needle tip to the rear of your work (not passing between the needle tips).

 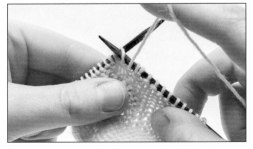

3 Bring the yarn to the front of the work between the needle tips, ready to work the next stitch.

4 Purl the next stitch as required. Work over the yarn over on the following row as described in steps 4–6 of *Working a yarn over between two knit stitches*.

WORKING A YARN OVER AFTER A KNIT AND BEFORE A PURL

1 Work in pattern until you reach the first yarn over instruction. Your yarn will be at the rear of your work.

2 Bring the yarn to the front of your work between the needle tips.

3 Bring the yarn over the right needle tip, so that it returns to the rear of your work. Bring the yarn to the front of your work between the needle tips once more.

4 Purl the next stitch as required. Work over the yarn over on the following row as described in steps 4–6 of *Working a yarn over between two knit stitches*.

WORKING A YARN OVER AFTER A PURL AND BEFORE A KNIT

1 Work in pattern until you reach the first yarn over instruction. Your yarn will be at the front of your work. Take the yarn over the needle to the rear of the work.

2 Knit the next stitch as required. Work over the yarn over on the following row as described in steps 4–6 of *Working a yarn over between two knit stitches*.

ALTERNATIVE METHOD FOR WORKING A YARN OVER AFTER A PURL AND BEFORE A KNIT

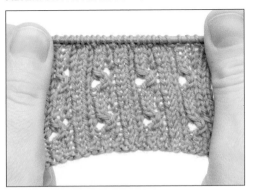

1 Have you ever noticed that some of your yarn overs are smaller than others? In this swatch 20 rows of the following stitch pattern have been worked:
Rows 1-4: 2x1 rib.
Row 5 (RS): P1, *k2, p1, k2tog, yo, p1; rep from * to last 3 sts, k2, p1.
Row 6: 2x1 rib.
Row 7: P1, *k2, p1, yo, ssk, p1; rep from * to last 3 sts, k2, p1.
Row 8: 2x1 rib.

The yarn over holes on row 5 are worked after a knit and before a purl, whereas the yarn over holes on row 7 are worked after a purl and before a knit. The row 7 holes are barely visible in comparison to the row 5 holes. The yarn overs that occur after a purl and before a knit are smaller as the yarn has only had to travel over the needle rather than right around it. You can adjust the size of the yarn overs worked after a purl and before a knit by working the following steps.

2 Work in pattern until you reach the first yarn over instruction. Your yarn will be at the front of your work.

3 Take the yarn to the rear of the work between the needle tips.

4 Bring the yarn over the right needle tip to the front of the work, then take the yarn to the rear of the work between the needle tips once more.

5 Knit the next stitch as instructed.

6 When you come to work over this yarn over on the following row you will see that the stitch is mounted on the needle back to front. That's to say that the leading leg of the stitch is at the rear of the needle rather than the front.

7 In order to work into the yarn over to keep the hole open, you will need to work the stitch through the back loop (either by knitting or purling as the pattern directs). In this example the yarn over is purled through the back loop.

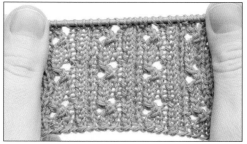

8 In this swatch 24 rows of the stitch pattern given in step 1 have been worked, but this time the yarn overs on row 7 of the pattern have been worked following this alternative method. You can clearly see that the row 7 yarn overs are now well-matched for size to the row 5 yarn overs, since the path travelled by the yarn is more similar for the two situations.

WORKING A YARN OVER AT THE START OF A ROW

1 Holding the needle tips parallel, pass the working yarn (attached to the left needle tip) over the right needle tip.

2 Keeping the yarn over the right needle tip, insert the right needle into the first stitch on the left needle and knit it.

3 You now have a yarn over loop on your needle in front of the first knitted stitch.

4 When you work back the next row, knit or purl the yarn over at the end in the normal way.

5 This creates an attractive looped edge.

READING LACE CHARTS

While it is entirely possible to work lace patterning from either written or charted instructions, a chart provides lots of extra information on how your pattern should appear and can make it easier and faster to spot errors. Wherever possible, the patterns we publish will include both written and charted instructions. However, as you work more complex designs, it often becomes impossible to include both, in which case most publications will include only the charted version of the design.

Each chart aims to systematically represent the right side of your knitting. You should be able to see at a glance whether your lace pattern is worked on a stocking stitch or on a garter stitch background. On a stocking stitch chart (chart A below) the majority of the chart squares will be blank to indicate that they are knitted on right side rows and purled on wrong side rows. This mimics stocking stitch fabric, which is smooth. On a garter stitch chart (chart B below) alternate rows have "purl bump dots" to indicate that these stitches are *knitted* on wrong side rows. This sometimes causes confusion as people strongly associate those dots with purling, however, knitting on the wrong side creates a purl bump on the right side of your fabric, and the chart represents how the fabric looks *on the right side*.

Basic Lace Techniques

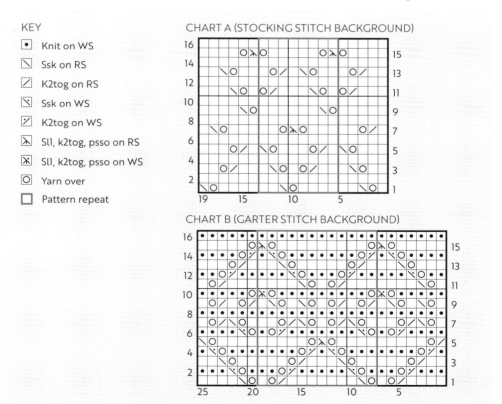

KEY

• Knit on WS

◺ Ssk on RS

◿ K2tog on RS

◿ Ssk on WS

◿ K2tog on WS

⋏ Sl1, k2tog, psso on RS

⋎ Sl1, k2tog, psso on WS

O Yarn over

☐ Pattern repeat

CHART A (STOCKING STITCH BACKGROUND)

CHART B (GARTER STITCH BACKGROUND)

All of the patterns in this volume are knitted flat, which means that right side and wrong side rows alternate. When you read a chart for working flat, you read right side rows from right to left, and wrong side rows from left to right. Generally, the row number will be located at the start of the row on the side where you start reading (so right side row numbers are on the right of the chart and wrong side row numbers are on the left of the chart). This is demonstrated on chart C below, where the row numbers are at each side of the chart.

You then read the symbols across the row of stitches in the order in which they appear.

Each symbol can represent either one stitch (as a knit or purl symbol does), or tell you what to do with a group of stitches (as the symbols for k2tog, ssk or cdd do), or even tell you how to increase a stitch without using an existing stitch (as you would when working a yarn over or M1 increase). The number of squares across the row represents how many stitches you will have on your needles at the *end* of the row (each of the examples above – knit, purl, k2tog, ssk, cdd, yo and M1 – results in one new stitch on your right needle).

KEY

☐ Knit on RS, purl on WS

• Purl on RS, knit on WS

◨ Ssk

◨ K2tog

◨ Sl1, k2tog, psso

◉ Yarn over

☐ Pattern repeat

CHART C (MADEIRA LACE)

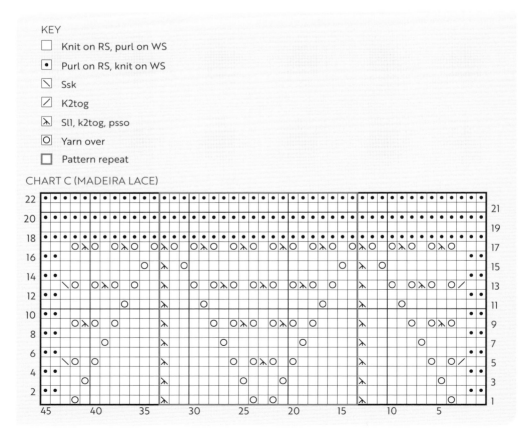

TECHNIQUE **READING LACE CHARTS**

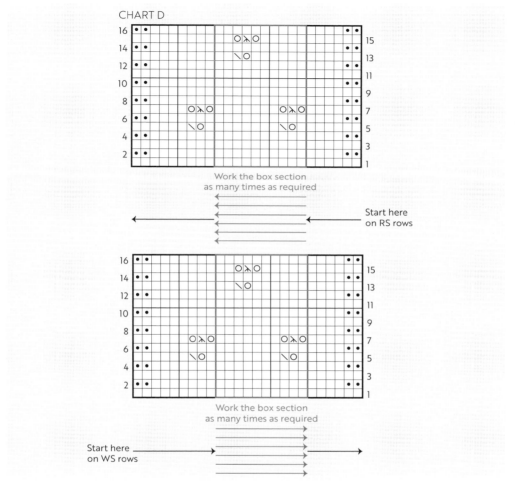

Often in lace designs, it is unnecessary to chart the entire row of knitting because a section of the pattern is repeated. In these cases, the chart will show a highlighted pattern repeat box. We usually mark the repeat with a red box, as in charts A–D.

When working across a right side row on this type of chart, you work the stitches on the right-hand end of the chart up to the repeat box. You then work the repeat box as many times as necessary, before completing the row with the stitches at the left-hand end of the chart row.

On the wrong side, you read from left to right and work the stitches at the left-hand end of the row, before repeating the section marked by the box as many times as necessary, and finally completing the row with the stitches to the right of the repeat box.

NO STITCH SYMBOLS

One of the elements of lace charts that can cause the most confusion is the "no stitch" symbol. Usually shown as a grey square, the no stitch is used to force a chart to line up in the way that your knitting will. Imagine for example a piece of 2x2 ribbing that has a droplet shape inserted in it. You work an increase in the centre of the purl rib, followed by two increases on the following row. The rest of the ribbing stays exactly the same, but you now have 3 extra stitches in your fabric. Without a no stitch symbol, the increased stitches would force the rib on the rows above to look like it was no longer lined up (as shown in chart E).

When you work from a chart with no stitch symbols, essentially you completely ignore them. Work across the row of instructions, reading only the knitting symbols and skipping over the grey squares. You can then stop and check your work at the end of the row, ensuring that your pattern is lined up in the way that you would expect. Chart F shows how the same pattern looks with no stitch symbols keeping the rib correctly lined up. Sometimes the need for no stitch symbols can be removed by "cutting out" the chart outline. This is demonstrated in chart G.

BUT BEWARE...

Unfortunately there isn't one fixed convention for charting knitting patterns. I have often longed for a knitting version of the IUPAC (International Union of Pure and Applied Chemistry) who were set up in 1919 to ensure standardisation of nomenclature, weights, measures, names and symbols in chemistry. This cooperation has led to much easier international communication within chemistry, and a similar coming together of the knitting industry would undoubtedly lead to a better experience for knitters, but sadly does not exist. This means that many

different symbols are used when charting knitting patterns, and not all charts follow the same rules, so please take care to read any chart notes and keys carefully before starting work.

CHART E (WITHOUT NO-STITCH SYMBOLS)

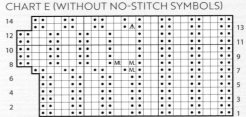

CHART F (WITH NO-STITCH SYMBOLS)

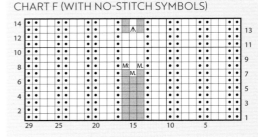

CHART G (CUTOUT CHART)

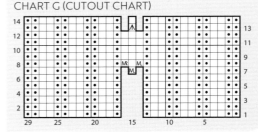

USING LACE CHARTS TO READ YOUR KNITTING

Learning to read your knitting is a vital tool in the quest for knitting confidence. Once you can see how your pattern and stitches should look, you are far less likely to make mistakes and face the frustration of ripping out hours of painstaking work.

The fastest way to get a feel for a lace design from its chart is to look for the yarn over holes. These are shown on the chart by a small circle, and you can compare the pattern created on the chart with the pattern created in the knitted red Myrtle lace swatch.

MYRTLE LACE

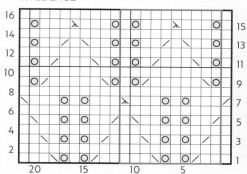
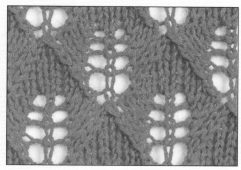

The next important feature on a lace chart is the decreases. These can be single decreases, in which case they will lean either right (k2tog shown as a right-leaning diagonal line on the chart) or they will lean to the left (there are various options for left-leaning decreases, but the patterns in this volume all use the ssk decrease and it's shown as a left-leaning diagonal line on the chart). The chart should give you a clear view of how these decreases line up with each other as the pattern is worked. This is demonstrated in the blue zigzag lace swatch and its accompanying chart.

ZIGZAG LACE

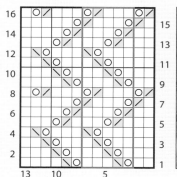

Alternatively, two yarn over holes can be balanced with a double decrease. There are various options for these, depending on the desired effect – they can be right-leaning (k3tog is the most common), left-leaning (often worked as sssk or sl1, k2tog, psso) or centred (cdd and s2sk are both used in this volume). The grey Horseshoe Lace swatch below and its chart feature left-leaning double decreases.

One of the most effective ways to avoid errors in your lace knitting is to stop at the end of each section and look back over your work. Are the holes and decreases lining up as you are expecting them to, from looking at the chart? Many lace patterns will be symmetrical, and as a result they will have a central stitch or pair of stitches that should always line up over each other. Look out for these features and try to notice as you work over them, and see whether your current row is correctly aligned. If the worst does happen, and you spot an error, refer to the tutorials starting on page 32 on fixing mistakes in your lace.

HORSESHOE LACE

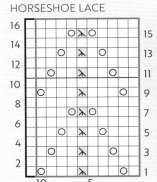

Donna Smith's pretty Aphaca scarf and blanket patterns are a great introduction to lace knitting. The central panel is particularly simple, requiring only that you keep track of your rows so that the eyelet pattern appears regularly. The edging lace pattern is known as Madeira Lace and gives a gently scalloped edge to the scarf and blanket.

PROJECT
APACA SCARF AND BLANKET

by Donna Smith

SIZES
Scarf (Small Blanket, Medium Blanket, Large Blanket)
Width: 29.5 (74.5, 92.5, 110.5) cm [11½ (29¼, 36¼, 43½) in]
Length: 159.5 (79.5, 111.5, 146.5) cm [62¾ (31¼, 44, 57¾) in]

YARN
Something to Knit With 4ply (70% highland wool, 30% superfine alpaca; 187m [205yds] per 50g skein)
3 (4, 7, 11) x 50g skeins
Scarf shown in Mist
Small blanket shown in Beach

NEEDLES AND NOTIONS
1 pair 3.75mm [US 5] knitting needles, or needle size required to match tension
Stitch markers (optional)
Wires and/or pins, or your preferred kit for blocking lace

TENSION
20 sts over Madeira Lace pattern (chart A) measures 9cm [3½in]
72 rows of Madeira Lace pattern (chart A) measures 22cm [8¾in] at its deepest
20 sts over Triplet Lace pattern (chart B) measures 9cm [3½in]
30 rows over Triplet Lace (chart B) pattern measures 10cm [4in]
All tension information is for swatches that have relaxed after washing and blocking.

ABBREVIATIONS
A full abbreviations list can be found on page 72.

PATTERN NOTES

This scarf and blanket are worked back and forth, starting with the Madeira Lace edging. For the scarf, the body pattern is then worked to half the length of the piece, before the stitches are left on hold. A second piece is then worked separately and grafted to the main part of the scarf. For the blanket sizes, the body pattern is worked to almost the length of the piece, before a second lace edging is worked, and the two sections are grafted together. This ensures that both ends of the fabric are symmetrical. Two stitches on either side are knitted in garter stitch to create a narrow border.

Steps 1–3 of the pattern are for working from charted instructions, and steps 4–6 are for working from written instructions. The scarf or blanket is then finished by following the instructions in step 7.

SPECIAL TECHNIQUES

Photo tutorials for the following techniques can be found within this book.

Working yarn overs (page 7)
Reading lace charts (page 13)
Blocking lace (page 46)

The following video tutorials may be found on our website at **www.acknitwear.co.uk/ something-new-to-learn-about-lace**

Working yarn overs
Grafting in stocking stitch (Kitchener stitch)
Grafting in garter stitch
Blocking lace

SCHEMATICS

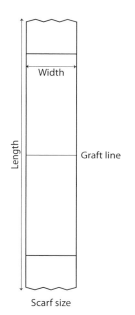

Width

Length

Graft line

Scarf size

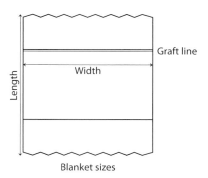

Graft line

Width

Length

Blanket sizes

Chapter 1

KEY

- ☐ Knit on RS, purl on WS
- ⦁ Purl on RS, knit on WS
- ◩ Ssk
- ◪ K2tog
- ⋋ Sll, k2tog, psso
- ⊙ Yarn over
- ☐ Pattern repeat

CHART B
TRIPLET LACE CENTRE

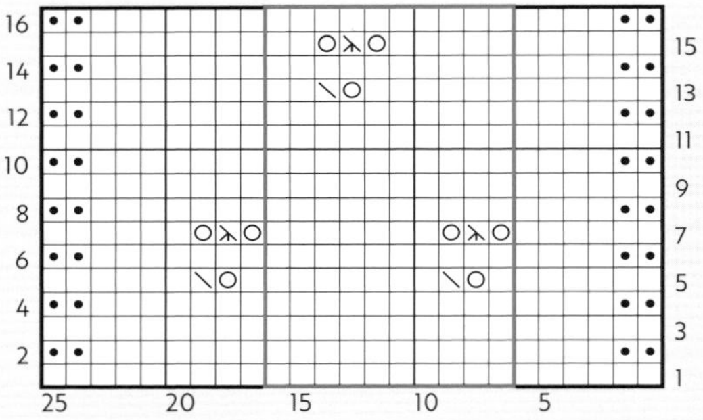

CHART A
MADEIRA LACE EDGING

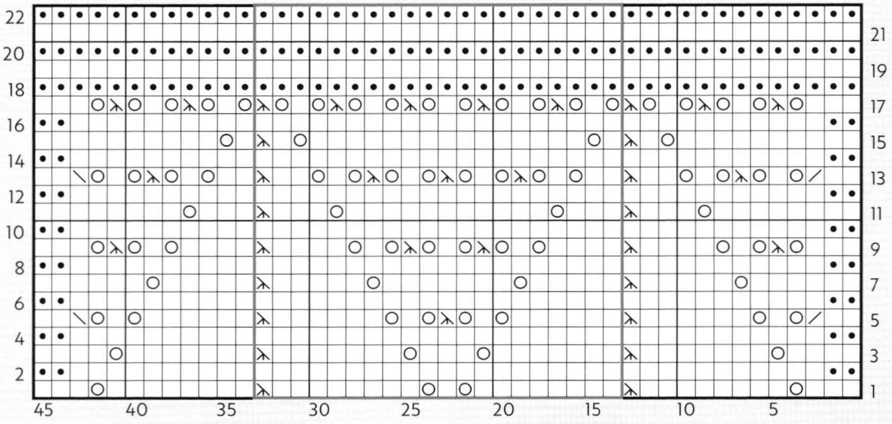

1 MADEIRA LACE EDGING –
CHARTED INSTRUCTIONS
Move to step 4 for written instructions.

Cast on 65 (165, 205, 245) sts.
Knit 6 rows.

Row 1 (RS): Reading from right to left,
work across row 1 of chart A, repeating the
marked section 2 (7, 9, 11) times in total.
Row 2 (WS): Reading from left to right,
work across row 2 of chart A, repeating the
marked section 2 (7, 9, 11) times in total.
Last 2 rows set chart A pattern. Working next
row of chart each time, cont as set until
chart A row 22 has been worked for the 3rd
(3rd, 3rd, 4th) time.

2 TRIPLET LACE CENTRE –
CHARTED INSTRUCTIONS
Row 1 (RS): Reading from right to
left, work across row 1 of chart B,
repeating the marked section 5
(15, 19, 23) times in total.
Row 2 (WS): Reading from left to
right, work across row 2 of chart
B, repeating the marked section 5
(15, 19, 23) times in total.
Last 2 rows set chart B pattern.
Working next row of chart each
time, cont as set until chart B row
1 (11, 11, 11) has been worked for
the 12th (7th, 13th, 17th) time.

Leave the sts on a needle or
waste yarn while you work on the
second lace edging.

3 SECOND MADEIRA LACE EDGING
– CHARTED INSTRUCTIONS
Cast on 65 (165, 205, 245) sts.
Knit 6 rows.

Row 1 (RS): Reading from right
to left, work across row 1 of chart

A, repeating the marked section 2 (7, 9, 11)
times in total.
Row 2 (WS): Reading from left to right,
work across row 2 of chart A, repeating the
marked section 2 (7, 9, 11) times in total.
Last 2 rows set chart A pattern. Working next
row of chart each time, cont as set until
chart A row 22 has been worked for the 3rd
(3rd, 3rd, 4th) time.

SCARF SIZE ONLY
Work step 2 once more, ending after working
chart B row 9 for the 11th time.

ALL SIZES
Move to step 7.

PROJECT **APHACA SCARF & BLANKET**

4 MADEIRA LACE EDGING –
WRITTEN INSTRUCTIONS

Cast on 65 (165, 205, 245) sts.
Knit 6 rows.

Row 1 (RS): K3, *yo, k8, sl1, k2tog, psso, k8, yo, k1; rep from * to last 2 sts, k2.
Row 2 (WS): K2, purl to last 2 sts, k2.
Row 3: K4, *yo, k7, sl1, k2tog, psso, k7, yo, k3; rep from * to last st, k1.
Row 4: As row 2.
Row 5: K2, k2tog, yo, k1, *yo, k6, sl1, k2tog, psso, k6, yo, k1, yo, sl1, k2tog, psso, yo, k1; rep from * to last 20 sts, yo, k6, sl1, k2tog, psso, k6, yo, k1, yo, ssk, k2.
Row 6: As row 2.
Row 7: K6, *yo, k5, sl1, k2tog, psso, k5, yo, k7; rep from * to last 19 sts, yo, k5, sl1, k2tog, psso, k5, yo, k6.
Row 8: As row 2.
Row 9: K3, *yo, sl1, k2tog, psso, yo, k1, yo, k4, sl1, k2tog, psso, k4, yo, k1, yo, sl1, k2tog, psso, yo, k1; rep from * to last 2 sts, k2.
Row 10: As row 2.
Row 11: K8, *yo, k3, sl1, k2tog, psso, k3, yo, k11; rep from * to last 17 sts, yo, k3, sl1, k2tog, psso, k3, yo, k8.
Row 12: As row 2.
Row 13: K2, k2tog, yo, k1, yo, sl1, k2tog, psso, yo, k1, *yo, k2, sl1, k2tog, psso, k2, yo, [k1, yo, sl1, k2tog, psso, yo] 3 times, k1; rep from * to last 16 sts, yo, k2, sl1, k2tog, psso, k2, yo, k1, yo, sl1, k2tog, psso, yo, k1, yo, ssk, k2.
Row 14: As row 2.
Row 15: K10, *yo, k1, sl1, k2tog, psso, k1, yo, k15; rep from * to last 15 sts, yo, k1, sl1, k2tog, psso, k1, yo, k10.
Row 16: As row 2.
Row 17: K3, *yo, sl1, k2tog, psso, yo, k1; rep from * to last 2 sts, k2.
Rows 18–22: Knit 5 rows.
Rep last 22 rows a further 2 (2, 2, 3) times.

5 TRIPLET LACE CENTRE –
WRITTEN INSTRUCTIONS

Row 1 (RS): Knit.
Row 2 and all foll WS rows: K2, purl to last 2 sts, k2.
Rows 3: As row 1.
Row 5: K7, *yo, ssk, k8; rep from * to last 8 sts, yo, ssk, k6.
Row 7: K6, *yo, sl1, k2tog, psso, yo, k7; rep from * to last 9 sts, yo, sl1, k2tog, psso, yo, k6.
Rows 9 & 11: As row 1.
Row 13: K12, *yo, ssk, k8; rep from * to last 3 sts, k3.
Row 15: K11, *yo, sl1, k2tog, psso, yo, k7; rep from * to last 4 sts, k4.
Row 16: As row 2.
Rep last 16 rows a further 10 (5, 11, 15) times.

SCARF SIZE ONLY
Work row 1 once more.

BLANKET SIZES
Work rows 1–11 once more.

ALL SIZES
Leave the sts on a needle or waste yarn while you work on the second lace edging.

6 SECOND LACE EDGING –
WRITTEN INSTRUCTIONS

Work step 4 once more, to create a second lace edging.

SCARF SIZE ONLY
Work step 5 once more, ending after row 9 has been worked for the 11th time.

ALL SIZES
Move to step 7.

7 FINISHING

Return the sts of your first piece to the needles.

With the wrong sides of both pieces facing each other, graft the live stitches together as follows:

Graft the first 2 sts together in garter stitch.

Graft the following sts in stocking stitch until 2 sts remain on each needle.

Graft the last 2 sts together in garter stitch.

Weave in all ends but do not trim.

Soak your scarf or blanket in lukewarm water and wool wash for 20 minutes. Squeeze out excess water (but do not wring). Press between towels to dry further. Lay your scarf or blanket flat to dry, threading wires or strong cotton along the straight garter stitch edges and pinning out the peaks of the lace edging. Stretch the fabric firmly in all directions to open up the lace patterns. Check that the edges are parallel by measuring the width at different points. When the scarf or blanket is completely dry, trim any remaining ends.

SOMETHING NEW TO LEARN ABOUT **LACE**

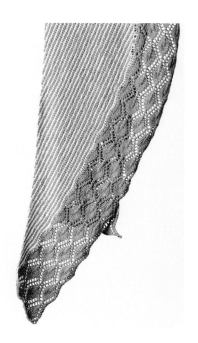

Chapter Two

TUTORIALS:
FIXING MISTAKES

PROJECT

DESIGNED BY **Martina Behm**

FIXING MISTAKES

It is better to learn how to avoid mistakes than to have to fix them. This chapter will take you through some methods for keeping track of your pattern, followed by techniques for correcting some of the most common errors in lace knitting. At the end of the chapter you will find Martina Behm's lovely Nissolia shawl pattern. This pretty design features a simple striped garter stitch centre, with a leaf motif knitted-on lace edging. The leaf pattern has strong, clear lines that will help you to quickly spot and fix any errors in your knitting.

USING STITCH MARKERS

Whilst you can buy all sorts of gloriously beautiful stitch markers, I find that for lace, the most useful are the small, unbroken ring markers, since they don't easily get caught in your stitches.

As a beginner lace knitter I found stitch markers absolutely invaluable. I use them less these days as I'm more able to read my knitting, but if I'm struggling to establish a stitch pattern, or making a repeated error, the first thing I do is to add markers around each repeat.

But how does adding stitch markers help? The most obvious way to spot that there's a problem in your lace pattern is that there are too few or too many stitches remaining at the end of the row. If you have stitch markers in place, the first check is to count how many stitches you have between each pair of markers. In almost every case, there will be a section with too many or too few stitches, and this will be the cause of the problem.

The second way in which markers can be helpful is to anchor you to features within the lace pattern. In the example of the Horseshoe Lace on page 18, if you place markers at the pattern repeat box lines, the marker is always after the central stitch, and the pattern is symmetrical either side of that. As you work along the row, you can keep an eye out for that symmetry – have you got 2 stitches each side of the central stitch between the decreases?

PLACING MARKERS

When deciding how to place markers in your knitting, first look at the chart. For a marker to stay in the same place in your work, and therefore be useful on multiple rows, it needs to enclose all of the paired increases and decreases in the stitch pattern repeat. Looking back at the charts on preceding pages, the Horseshoe Lace on page 18 will be easily mastered by placing markers at the pattern repeat box lines. Each repeat of that box works the double decrease (sl1, k2tog, psso) as well as both of the balancing yarn overs on all rows of the pattern. However, if you look at the Zigzag Lace chart on page 17, this is not the case. Rows 1–6 work fine if you add markers at the pattern repeat box lines, but on row 7 the marker lies between the k2tog and its yarn over. When you work along this row, the marker will be in the centre of the 2 stitches that you should be knitting together. You can either overcome this by completely removing the markers as you work this row and then replacing them on row 8, or by moving them as you go, replacing them after the k2tog is completed. A similar difficulty occurs with the Myrtle Lace pattern also on page 17, where rows 7 and 23 find the decreases and their yarn overs divided by the pattern repeat lines.

ADDING A LIFELINE

The best way to "back up" your progress on a lace project is to add a lifeline to your work. A lifeline is a piece of waste yarn that is threaded through all of the stitches on a row (but not any stitch markers!). If you make a mistake above the lifeline and are unable to fix it in any other way, you can take your needles out of your work and rip back to the lifeline. At that point you will have all of your stitches held safely, and you can thread them back onto your needles. If you are finding a lace pattern hard to keep straight, it may be worth adding a lifeline after each complete row repeat of the pattern.

1 Thread a length of smooth cotton onto a tapestry needle. If you are working on circular needles, move the stitches onto the cable and thread the cotton through each stitch.

2 If you are working on straight needles, it may not be possible to thread the tapestry needles through the stitches, in which case, slip the stitches off the knitting needle, onto the waste yarn.

3 Then you just need to return the stitches to the needles, leaving the waste yarn in place.

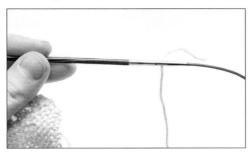

4 Some interchangeable circular needles have a small hole in the barrel. Thread a length of waste yarn through the hole in the right-hand needle.

5 As the following row is worked, the lifeline passes through all of the stitches.

Fixing Mistakes

READING YOUR KNITTING TO FIND AN ERROR

If you come to the end of your row, and have too many or too few stitches remaining for the completion of the pattern, there must be an error somewhere. Firstly look generally at your fabric, to see whether there is an obvious mistake in the lace patterning – a missing yarn over, or the line of holes or decreases isn't lying correctly. Compare your fabric to the chart, particularly looking for symmetrical elements. If the mistake is a row or two down your work, it is likely to be immediately obvious and you should mark it with a locking stitch marker or safety pin.

RECOGNISING STITCHES

To spot where your mistake is, you need to be able to recognise stitches on your needles. The following images show how some of the most common lace stitches appear.

If you aren't able to instantly see the mistake, you may have made an error on your current row. In this case you will need to work along the row looking for the errant stitch or group of stitches. If you are using stitch markers, count the stitches between each repeat, as this may help to isolate the problem. Without stitch markers you will need to read your way along the row, comparing your stitches to the instructions and looking at each stitch, checking whether it is a knit, purl, yarn over, k2tog, ssk, double decrease, or some other stitch. When you locate the problem, mark the mistake with a locking stitch marker or safety pin.

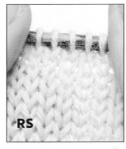 

1 A knit stitch has a "purl bump loop" at the rear of the needles, and sits nearly perpendicular across the needle.

2 A purl stitch has the purl bump loop at the front of the needles and also sits close to perpendicular across the needle.

3 A yarn over sits more diagonally across the needles, and doesn't have a purl bump loop at either side of the needle.

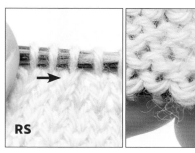

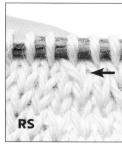

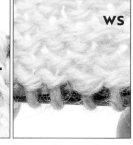

4 A k2tog decrease has two loops in the purl bump loop at the rear of the needle, and you can see that the stitches on the right side are leaning to the right.

5 An ssk decrease has two purl bump loops at the rear of the needle, and the stitches on the right side lean to the left.

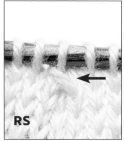

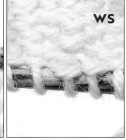

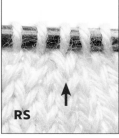

6 A sl1, k2tog, psso double decrease has a distinctive look on the right side of the fabric, you can see the slipped stitch lying over the k2tog, and the slipped stitch leans to the left. At the rear of the needle you should be able to see 3 loops sitting at the base of the stitch.

7 Both cdd and s2sk are centred double decreases, and have a very similar appearance. At the rear of the needle you will find 3 loops sitting at the base of the stitch, whilst on the right side there is a more prominent central stitch that sits forward from the rest of the fabric and lies straight.

HOW TO FIX THE MISTAKE

Once you have located the cause of the problem, mark it with a locking stitch marker before deciding on which course of action to take. The simplest solution is to ignore the error and move on, adjusting the stitch count (by working an increase or decrease) as close to the cause of the problem as possible. Many errors are just not *that* noticeable in a large piece of knitting, particularly if you resist pointing them out to other people! Alternatively, if the mistake is either too big to ignore, or makes carrying on impossible, then you will need to correct it. The most common error in lace knitting is to forget to work a yarn over, and happily this is the most straightforward error to correct, since it doesn't even require undoing your work, as long as you spot it within a row or two.

PICKING UP A YARN OVER MISSED ON THE PREVIOUS ROW

1 Work in pattern until you reach the marker where your yarn over is missing.

2 Bring the tip of the left needle under the strand between stitches, from front to back.

3 Knit or purl into the front of this loop. Here the loop is being purled.

4 The resulting yarn over hole will be slightly smaller than one created on the correct row, but once the fabric is blocked it will be imperceptible.

PICKING UP A YARN OVER MISSED TWO ROWS BACK

If the project on which you are working has plain wrong side rows, you may not spot an error until you've worked a row over it. In this case you can still replace a missing yarn over, and again after blocking you are unlikely to be able to spot the location of the correction.

1 Work in pattern until you reach the marker where your yarn over is missing.

2 Bring the tip of the left needle under both the strand between stitches and the strand between stitches on the row below, picking them up from front to back. You will have two loops on your left needle tip.

3 Use the right needle tip to lift the lower strand over the upper one and off the needle.

4 This creates the missing yarn over and the purl from the following row.

5 Once the row is complete, it will be very hard to spot which yarn over was missing.

TINKING BACK TO CORRECT AN ERROR

If the mistake isn't a missing yarn over, and is on your current row, or the row before, it is likely easiest to tink back to the mistake and then correct it. Tinking is the process of unknitting stitches one by one – tink being knit written backwards.

TINKING KNIT STITCH(ES)

1 To tink stitches, you hold the needle with the working yarn in your right hand, with the yarn tensioned fairly firmly.

2 Insert your left needle tip into the stitch (or when tinking a k2tog, into the stitches) below the stitch on the right needle, going into the stitch so that the needle tip points along your working yarn towards the ball.

3 Carefully slip the stitch off your right needle.

4 Pull the working yarn out of the stitch that should now be sitting on your left needle. The working yarn is again attached to the last stitch on your right needle, and you can repeat the process until you reach the error.

TINKING A YARN OVER

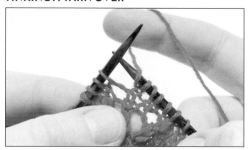

1 Any yarn overs will simply unwind off the needle as there is no stitch on the row below to "catch".

TINKING STITCHES WORKED THROUGH THE BACK LOOP

1 If a stitch has been worked through the back loop, like a k1 tbl or an ssk decrease, you will need to insert the left needle from back to front through the stitch(es) below the stitch on the right needle.

2 Slip the stitch off the right needle, and gently pull the working yarn out, leaving the stitch(es) on the left needle.

3 Having tinked an ssk, you will see that the stitches are mounted with the left leg at the front. Slip each stitch knitwise to the right needle to untwist them.

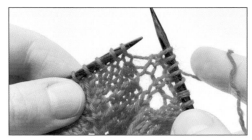

4 Return the two untwisted stitches to the left needle tip.

TINKING A SL1, K2TOG, PSSO

1 The slipped stitch from the double decrease sits across the k2tog, so lift the slipped stitch back up onto the right needle tip.

2 Tink the k2tog by inserting the left needle tip into the two stitches at the base of the first stitch on the right needle tip.

3 Remove the right needle from the stitch, leaving two stitches on the left needle tip.

4 Slip the first stitch on the right needle to the left needle. All three stitches are now on the left needle.

When you tink a stitch you are working it backwards. So to tink any stitch you need to think through the steps of making that stitch and then work through them in reverse in order to undo it. If you find it hard to imagine the stitch in reverse, work the next stitch without slipping the finished stitch off the needles. You can then look at your needle position and work out how it should be placed to unknit the stitch.

Tinking is a great method for correcting a small group of stitches that aren't too far back in your work. If the error is more than a couple of rows back, you will need a more drastic approach to fixing the error.

FIXING AN ERROR FURTHER BACK

If it's a large mistake and you have used a lifeline recently, you can remove the needles and gently pull our your knitting until you reach the lifeline, before returning the stitches to your needles.

DROPPING TO A LIFELINE

1 In this swatch a number of errors have been made and a lifeline was added at the end of the first pattern repeat. The mistakes can be removed by undoing the work back to the lifeline.

2 Remove the needles from your work.

3 Gently unravel your stitches, winding the yarn back onto the ball.

4 Once you reach your lifeline, slip the stitches back onto your needles, checking that you end up with the working yarn at the needle tip!

BLOCKING OUT AN ERROR

This solution isn't just about forgetting you ever made the mistake and vowing not to look at that section of the project ever again! It's about reshaping part of your knitting during the blocking process (see page 46 for detailed instructions on blocking). You would be surprised how effective it is to simply move the stitches with your fingers (and perhaps some help from a pin or an end of yarn) and leave them to dry.

1 In this swatch, a yarn over has been missed in the central spine section.

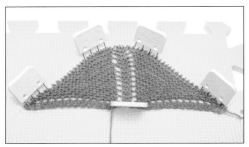

2 After the fabric has been soaked in warm water for 20 minutes, pin it flat to dry.

3 Use your fingers to create a hole where the yarn over is missing.

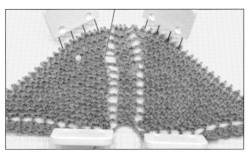

4 You can add pins to hold the hole open. Once dry it is much less obvious that there is an error in the knitting.

Hopefully you won't need to fix any errors as you work on Martina Behm's pretty Nissolia shawl, but why not try out adding a lifeline to your work? And practise reading your knitting even if everything is going to plan!

PROJECT
NISSOLIA SHAWL
by Martina Behm

SOMETHING NEW TO LEARN ABOUT **LACE**

SIZE
Width: 170cm [67in]
Depth: 39cm [15¼in]

YARN
Something to Knit With 4ply (70% highland wool, 30% superfine alpaca; 187m [205yds] per 50g skein)
Yarn A: Storm; 3 x 50g skeins
Yarn B: Cheeks; 1 x 50g skein

NEEDLES AND NOTIONS
1 set 4mm [US 6] circular needles, at least 80cm [32in] long, or needle size required to match tension
Stitch marker
Wires and/or pins, or your preferred kit for blocking lace

TENSION
18 sts and 42 rows to 10cm [4in] over garter stitch
34 sts of the Lace Edging pattern (at chart row 8, the widest point) measures 14cm [5½in]
20 rows of Lace Edging pattern measures 7cm [2¾in]
All tension information is for swatches that have relaxed after washing and blocking.

ABBREVIATIONS
s2sk   slip next 2 stitches as if to k2tog, slip next stitch knitwise, insert left needle into the front of all 3 slipped stitches and knit them together (2 stitches decreased)

w&t   wrap & turn; with yarn at back, slip next stitch purlwise from left to right needle, bring yarn to front between the needle tips, return slipped stitch to left needle, turn ready to work the next row leaving all remaining stitches unworked

A full abbreviations list can be found on page 72.

PATTERN NOTES
The centre of this shawl is worked on the bias in garter stitch stripes. There is no need to break the yarns between stripes. Leave the unused yarn at the RS while you work the other colour. To keep your edge neat, make sure you are consistent in how you pick up the yarn when you change colours – either pick up the new yarn from under the old, or from above, but stick with whichever you choose.

In the first section, the length of the rows being worked is increasing, followed by a second section where the row length remains constant. Throughout the centre of the shawl, stitches are being wrapped and left unworked (a process called short-row shaping). This process is simple to knit and creates an attractive trapezoid shape. Stitches are then cast on and a Leaf Lace edging is worked perpendicular to the centre stitches. This both attaches the edging and effectively casts off the centre stitches, leaving the join both neat and stretchy.

The wrap and turn method is used here to avoid holes, but the wraps are not picked up later on. The wrapped stitches are not knitted until the lace border is attached.

SPECIAL TECHNIQUES
Photo tutorials for the following techniques can be found within this book.
> **Working yarn overs (page 7)**
> **Reading lace charts (page 13)**
> **Blocking lace (page 46)**

The following video tutorials may be found on our website at **www.acknitwear.co.uk/ something-new-to-learn-about-lace**
> **Working yarn overs**
> **Adding a knitted-on edging**
> **Short rows in garter stitch (wrap and turn method)**
> **Blocking lace**

Chapter 2

SCHEMATIC

KEY

☐ Knit on RS, purl on WS

◩ Ssk

◪ K2tog

⊼ **S2sk** sl2 as if to k2tog, sl1 knitwise, insert left needle into all 3 slipped sts and knit them together

◖ **K2togE** knit together 1 edging stitch with 1 centre stitch

◯ Yarn over

☑ Sl1 purlwise with yarn in front

▨ No stitch, ignore these squares and move straight to next knitting instruction (see page 16)

❘ Slip marker

CHART
LEAF LACE EDGING

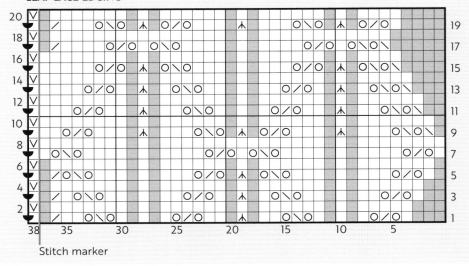

Stitch marker

1 STRIPED CENTRE, PART 1

Using yarn A, cast on 4 sts.

Set-up row 1 (RS): With yarn A, kfb, k2, w&t.
1 st inc; 5 sts.
Set-up row 2 (WS): With yarn A, k1, pm, k2,
kfb. *1 st inc; 6 sts (2 sts before the marker
and 4 sts after the marker).*

Row 1 (RS): With yarn B, kfb, knit to marker,
remove marker, w&t. *1 st inc.*
Row 2 (WS): With yarn B, k1, pm, knit to last
st, kfb. *1 st inc.*
Row 3: With yarn A, kfb, knit to marker,
remove marker, w&t. *1 st inc.*
Row 4: With yarn A, k1, pm, knit to last st,
kfb. *1 st inc.*
These 4 rows set the striped garter stitch
centre pattern. Note that in this section you
are increasing 1 st on every row, and making
a new wrapped st on every other row. The
marker allows you to easily see where to
work to on each RS row.

Rep these 4 rows a further 52 times. *212
sts inc; 218 sts. You should now have 107
wrapped sts and 111 unwrapped sts (1 of
which is on the same side of the marker as
the wrapped sts).*

Rep rows 1 & 2 once more. *2 sts inc; 220 sts.*

2 STRIPED CENTRE, PART 2

Row 1 (RS): With yarn A, kfb, knit to marker,
remove marker, w&t. *1 st inc.*
Row 2 (WS): With yarn A, k2, pm, knit to last
st, kfb. *1 st inc.*
Row 3: With yarn B, kfb, knit to marker,
remove marker, w&t. *1 st inc.*
Row 4: With yarn B, k2, pm, knit to last st,
kfb. *1 st inc.*
These 4 rows set the second part of the
striped garter stitch centre pattern. Note
that in this section, you are still increasing 1

st on every row, but instead of the wrapped
sts being adjacent to each other, they now
alternate with unwrapped sts. This means
that the number of sts you are knitting on
each row remains constant.

Rep these 4 rows a further 14 times, without
placing the stitch marker in the final row. *60
sts inc; 280 sts.*

Break yarn B, leaving a tail to weave in later.
If desired, place a lifeline through all sts.

Move to step 3 for charted instructions or step
4 for written instructions for the lace edging.

3 KNITTED-ON LEAF LACE EDGING –
CHARTED INSTRUCTIONS

The knitted-on edging is worked in yarn A
only.
Using yarn A (which is still attached to your
knitting), and the backwards-loop method,
cast on 1 st to your left needle, pm, cast on a
further 26 sts to your left needle. *27 edging
sts and 280 centre sts.*

Throughout the following section, 1 edging st
remains on the centre sts side of the marker.

Row 1 (RS): Reading from right to left, work
across row 1 of chart. *1 edging st inc and 1
centre st dec.*
Row 2 (WS): Reading from left to right, work
across row 2 of chart.
Last 2 rows set knitted-on lace edging
pattern. The edging stitch count changes on
each row. For more detailed stitch counts,
please refer to the written instructions in step
4. Cont to work from chart until row 19 has
been completed for the 28th time. All centre
sts have now been consumed. *27 sts remain.*
Cast off all sts purlwise.

Move to step 5.

4 KNITTED-ON LEAF LACE EDGING – WRITTEN INSTRUCTIONS

The knitted-on edging is worked in yarn A only.

Using yarn A (which is still attached to your knitting), and the backwards-loop method, cast on 1 st to your left needle, pm, cast on a further 26 sts to your left needle. *27 edging sts and 280 centre sts.*

Throughout the following section, 1 edging st remains on the centre sts side of the marker.

Row 1 (RS): K1, yo, k2tog, yo, k3, yo, ssk, yo, k2, s2sk, k2, yo, k2tog, yo, k3, yo, ssk, yo, k2, k2tog, slm, k2togE. *1 edging st inc; 28 edging sts; 1 centre st dec.*

Row 2 and all following WS rows: Sl1, slm, purl to end.

Row 3: K1, yo, k2tog, yo, k5, yo, ssk, yo, k1, s2sk, k1, yo, k2tog, yo, k5, yo, ssk, yo, k1, k2tog, slm, k2togE. *1 edging st inc; 29 edging sts; 1 centre st dec.*

Row 5: K1, yo, k2tog, yo, k7, yo, ssk, yo, s2sk, yo, k2tog, yo, k7, yo, ssk, yo, k2tog, slm, k2togE. *1 edging st inc; 30 edging sts; 1 centre st dec.*

Row 7: [K1, yo, k2tog, yo, k9, yo, ssk, yo] twice, k1, slm, k2togE. *4 edging sts inc; 34 edging sts; 1 centre st dec.*

Row 9: [Ssk, yo] twice, k3, s2sk, k3, yo, k2tog, yo, s2sk, yo, ssk, yo, k3, s2sk, k3, yo, k2tog, yo, k2, slm, k2togE. *3 edging sts dec; 31 edging sts; 1 centre st dec.*

Row 11: [Ssk, yo] twice, k2, s2sk, k2, yo, k2tog, yo, k3, yo, ssk, yo, k2, s2sk, k2, yo, k2tog, yo, k3, slm, k2togE. *1 edging st dec; 30 edging sts; 1 centre st dec.*

Row 13: [Ssk, yo] twice, k1, s2sk, k1, yo, k2tog, yo, k5, yo, ssk, yo, k1, s2sk, k1, yo, k2tog, yo, k4, slm, k2togE. *1 edging st dec; 29 edging sts; 1 centre st dec.*

Row 15: [Ssk, yo] twice, s2sk, yo, k2tog, yo, k7, yo, ssk, yo, s2sk, yo, k2tog, yo, k5, slm, k2togE. *1 edging st dec; 28 edging sts; 1 centre st dec.*

Row 17: [Ssk, yo] twice, k1, yo, k2tog, yo, k9, yo, ssk, yo, k1, yo, k2tog, yo, k4, k2tog, slm, k2togE. *2 edging sts inc; 30 edging sts; 1 centre st dec.*

Row 19: K1, yo, k2tog, yo, s2sk, yo, ssk, yo, k3, s2sk, k3, yo, k2tog, yo, s2sk, yo, ssk, yo, k3, k2tog, slm, k2togE. *3 edging sts dec; 27 edging sts; 1 centre st dec.*

Row 20: As row 2.

Rep last 20 rows a further 26 times. *27 edging sts and 10 centre sts remain.*
Rep rows 1–19 once more. *27 edging sts remain.*

Cast off all sts purlwise.

5 FINISHING

Weave in all ends but do not trim.
Soak your shawl in lukewarm water and wool wash for 20 minutes. Squeeze out excess water (but do not wring). Press between towels to dry further. Lay your shawl flat to dry, threading wires or strong cotton along the straight upper edge and pinning out the peaks of the lace edging using either pins or wires. Stretch the fabric firmly in all directions to open up the lace patterns. When the shawl is completely dry, trim any remaining ends.

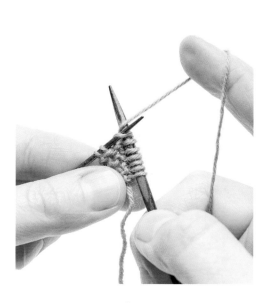

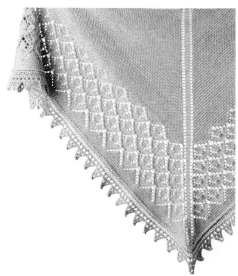

Chapter Three

PROJECT
DESIGNED BY **Jen Arnall-Culliford**

BLOCKING LACE

More than any other technique in knitting, lace is completely transformed by the simple process of soaking, stretching and leaving to dry. Many a new knitter has thought they have knitted their lace project completely wrong, because it looks like a hair net when it comes off the needles. Blocking is a completely transformative process. The following tutorials show you a range of different methods for blocking, including how to stretch different shaped shawls (square or rectangle, triangles and curved edges), and how to use different blocking kits (just pins, combs, wires and pins, or a blocking frame). Whichever kit

is used, you will need a space in which to stretch out your project. This can be a bed or floor area with a clean towel laid over it, or foam blocking mats, or even a full blocking frame. Any metal that comes into contact with your knitted fabric must be rust-proof (all wires and pins for example), otherwise rust marks can easily damage your work.

Blocking is to lace knitting as blow-drying is to hair. It uses the fact that soaking in water interrupts the hydrogen-bonding within and between the fibres, and when dry, the fibres or hair will re-bond and hold their new shape temporarily. As such, each time you wash a lace project it will need re-blocking.

1 Soak your fabric in hand-warm water with a small amount of wool wash, for at least 20 minutes.

2 Squeeze out excess water, but don't wring, since that can permanently damage the yarn. Then lay the shawl flat to dry.

USING PINS

Where the edges of your shawl should be straight, multiple pins will be required to prevent the edge from being scalloped. On purposefully scalloped edges, a single pin can be used at each point of the edge. It is well worth keeping a long ruler to hand, to ensure that edges are both straight and parallel.

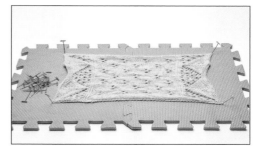

1 Pin out the corners of your shawl to the desired measurements.

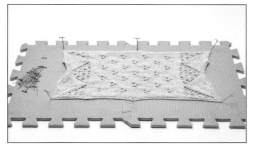

2 Divide each straight edge in half and pin.

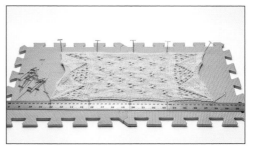

3 Divide each section in half again and pin.

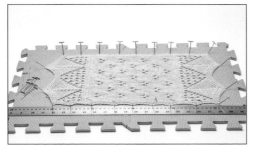

4 Continue to divide each section in half until the edges are lying straight. Pin each point of any scalloped edges and leave to dry.

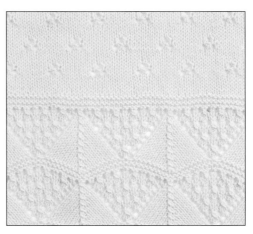

USING PIN COMBS

As an upgrade to using single pins, there are pin combs, which hold a number of pins in a straight line, thus speeding up the ability to stretch out a shawl and keep edges straight. These combs often include a hole that allows you to attach a strong thread that can be used to stretch out scalloped edges.

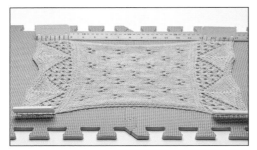

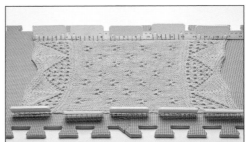

1 Use a comb to pin out the corners of the straight edges of the shawl.

2 Work along each edge, using the combs to stretch it out, ensuring that the sections between combs aren't distorted. Add extra combs or single pins if required.

3 Attach a strong thread to the comb at the corner and thread it through each point. Tie the thread to the comb at the opposite corner. Leave to dry.

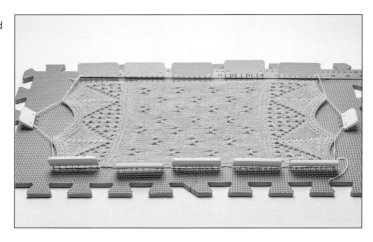

USING WIRES AND PINS

Using a combination of wires and pins saves a huge amount of time when blocking a large project. Threading a wire along a straight edge makes it far easier to keep the edge straight, and allows you to adjust how much you stretch it without having to undo hundreds of pins. You can also thread wires through the points of a scalloped edge, which again makes adjusting its position far easier than if each point were pinned separately. Both straight and flexible wires are available, depending on the shape of shawl you are blocking.

USING WIRES TO BLOCK A GARTER STITCH EDGE

Two options are available for how to block a garter stitch edge, depending on your desired effect.

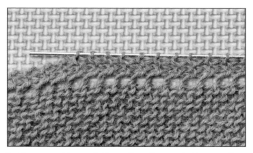

1 You can thread the wire through the ends of the garter ridges, passing under a purl bump each time.

2 This gives a smooth, straight finish to the edges.

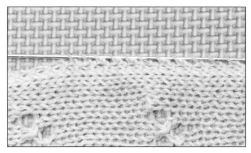

3 Alternatively, you can thread the wire through the longer stitches between ridges – taking care to always pass through the edge in the same direction.

4 This gives an attractive looped edging.

BLOCKING A TRIANGLE WITH WIRES

1 Thread wires along the edges of any straight edges, either following a column of yarn over holes, or working along the stitches at the edge of the fabric.

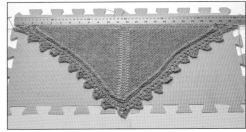

2 Use a ruler to check that straight edges are lying straight, and pin into place.

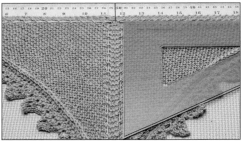

3 Thread wires along the central spine of your triangle (if it has one), and check that the spine is perpendicular to the top edge, using a set square. Pin the central point.

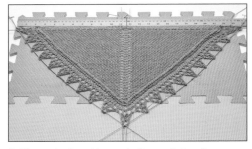

4 Thread wires through the points of any scalloped edges and pin in place.

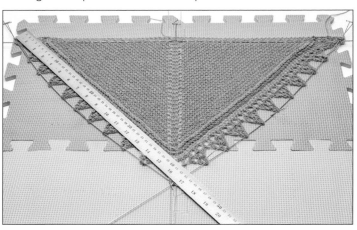

5 Check that symmetrical sides are of equal length, and the fabric of the shawl is lying evenly, with patterning lying straight where it should. Adjust where the wires are pinned if required, and leave to dry.

BLOCKING CURVED EDGES

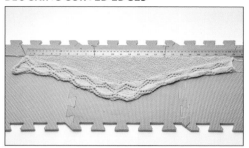

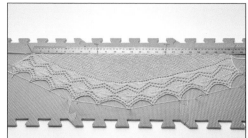

Flexible wires or strong cotton are most useful for blocking curved edges.

1 Block any straight edges using your preferred method.

2 Thread the curved edge with a wire or strong cotton tied at each end to a pin. Use pins to stretch the widest point of the curve. Add extra pins to ensure that the curved edge is smooth, and leave to dry.

USING A BLOCKING FRAME

If you are short of space, or make a large number of square and right-angled triangle shawls, then a blocking frame may be useful. These allow a shawl to be stretched and left leaning up against a wall to dry. You will find a full tutorial on blocking with a frame (also known as a hap stretcher) over on our blog.
www.acknitwear.co.uk/blog/2017/1/17/ how-to-use-a-hap-blocking-frame

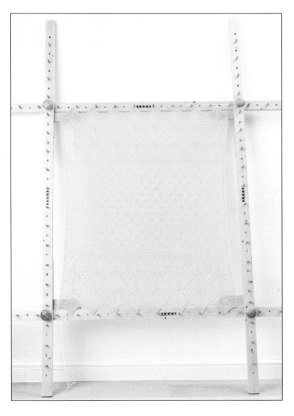

GARTER TAB CAST-ON METHOD

To reveal its true beauty, lace needs to be firmly blocked. Cast-on and cast-off edges are generally tighter than the surrounding fabric, and this can hamper blocking a piece to its full potential size. Whilst it is possible to simply use a stretchy cast on or cast off, knitters have created numerous inventive ways to entirely avoid these edges. One such method is the garter tab cast on, where a small strip of garter stitch is used to create 3 directions of knitting at once. This method is used for triangular shawls worked out from the centre back neck, such as my Bithynica shawl.

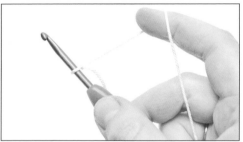

1 Make a slip knot in your waste yarn and place it on your crochet hook.

2 Hold the crochet hook over your knitting needle and pass the waste yarn under the knitting needle and over the crochet hook.

3 Pull the loop through the slip knot on the crochet hook. You now have 1 stitch on your knitting needle.

4 Pass the waste yarn under the knitting needle and over the crochet hook.

5 Pull the loop through the stitch on the crochet hook. Repeat steps 4 and 5 once more. You now have 3 stitches on your knitting needle.

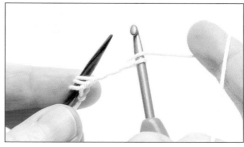

6 Work 3 more crochet chain stitches by passing the waste yarn over the hook and pulling the loop through, then fasten off.

7 Change to main yarn and knit 7 rows on these 3 stitches.

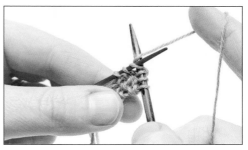

8 Turn your work through 90° and use a thin needle to pick up 3 stitches in the ends of the garter stitch ridges. Knit across these 3 stitches.

9 Pull the end of the waste yarn through the final chain stitch until the chain starts to unravel.

10 Gently pull on the end of the waste yarn to reveal the first main yarn stitch. Use a spare needle (you may find it easier with a smaller size needle) to pick up the main yarn stitches revealed, as you unzip the waste yarn.

Advanced Lace Techniques

11 The third stitch in the row will be the point where the yarn moved up to work the second row of knitting, and you may need to pull the end of the waste yarn out of this stitch. If your third stitch isn't on the waste yarn, pick up a loop from the corner of the fabric.

12 Knit across the 3 stitches from the cast-on edge.

13 You now have 9 stitches on your needles, and they are arranged ready to work in three perpendicular directions.

MAKING LARGER HOLES IN YOUR KNITTING
Some lace patterns require larger holes to be made in your fabric. The simplest method is to work a double yarn over. Double yarn overs are used in the Tulip Lace pattern and knitted-on lace edgings used in my Bithynica shawl design.

WORKING DOUBLE YARN OVERS

1 Work in pattern until you reach the first yarn over instruction. Your yarn will be at the rear of your work.

2 Bring the yarn to the front of your work between the needle tips.

3 Bring the yarn over the right needle tip, so that it returns to the rear of your work, then repeat steps 2 and 3 once more to create the second yarn over.

4 Work to the end of the row as required. You will see that the double yarn over has no purl bump at its base on either side (as there would be with a knit or purl).

WORKING INTO DOUBLE YARN OVERS

It isn't possible to work into both yarn over stitches in the same way (either both knits or both purls), so instead the second stitch is either worked through the back loop or one yarn over is knitted and the other purled or vice versa.

PURLING INTO DOUBLE YARN OVERS

1 Purl into the first yarn over.

2 Purl the second yarn over through the back loop.

ALTERNATIVE PURLING INTO DOUBLE YARN OVERS

1 Purl into the first yarn over as before, then knit into the second yarn over.

2 Once the double yarn over has been worked you can start to see the hole that it has created.

3 Having worked a few more rows, you can see the larger hole that has been made by the double yarn over.

KNITTING INTO DOUBLE YARN OVERS

1 Knit into the first yarn over.

ALTERNATIVE KNITTING INTO DOUBLE YARN OVERS

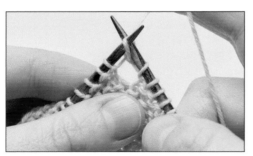

2 Knit the second yarn over through the back loop.

1 Knit into the first yarn over as before. Purl into the second yarn over.

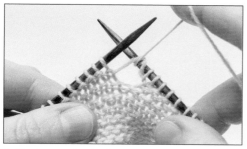

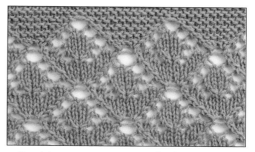

2 Having worked a few more rows, you can see the larger hole created by the double yarn over.

Double yarn overs are worked at the top of each tulip flower in my Bithynica shawl.

EVEN LARGER HOLES

If your design requires larger holes in your work, the simplest method is to add stitches using the backwards loop cast on at the point where the hole is required.

1 Work in pattern to the point where the hole is required.

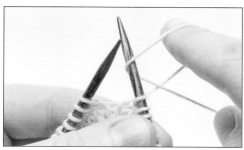

2 Make a loop over your finger and slip the loop onto your left needle tip.

3 Repeat step 2 until you have sufficient stitches cast on.

4 Work the next pattern stitch as directed.

5 When you work back on the following row or round, take care not to over-pull the stitches, so that the cast-on edge remains even.

6 Once you have worked a few more rows, you will be able to see the even larger hole in your fabric.

With a garter tab cast on and two pretty lace patterns, my Bithynica shawl will allow you to practise many of the skills in this book, as well as keeping you cosy all year round.

PROJECT
BITHYNICA SHAWL
by *Jen Arnall-Culliford*

Chapter 3

SOMETHING NEW TO LEARN ABOUT **LACE**

PROJECT **BITHYNICA SHAWL**

SIZE
Wingspan: 136cm [53½in]
Depth at centre: 68cm [26¾in]

YARN
Something to Knit With 4ply (70% highland wool, 30% superfine alpaca; 187m [205yds] per 50g skein)
Lawn: 4 x 50g skeins

NEEDLES AND NOTIONS
1 set 3.75mm [US 5] knitting needles (a circular needle may be required due to the number of stitches at the end of the shawl)
Stitch markers
Wires and/or pins, or your preferred kit for blocking lace

TENSION
21 sts and 38 rows to 10cm [4in] over centre garter stitch after washing and blocking
24 sts of Tulip Lace pattern measures 11cm [4¼in] after washing and blocking
32 rows of Tulip Lace pattern measures 10cm [4in] after washing and blocking
Lace edging at widest point measures 5.5cm [2¼in]

ABBREVIATIONS

ssk	slip 1 stitch knitwise, slip 1 stitch purlwise (or knitwise), return both stitches to left needle without twisting and knit them together through the back loop (1 stitch decreased)
sssk	slip 3 stitches separately, knitwise, return all 3 stitches to left needle without twisting and knit them together through the back loop (2 stitches decreased)
sskE	work as ssk, the first slipped stitch comes from the edging, and the second slipped stitch is a centre stitch, thus joining the edging to the centre of the shawl (1 centre stitch decreased)

A full abbreviations list can be found on page 72.

SCHEMATIC

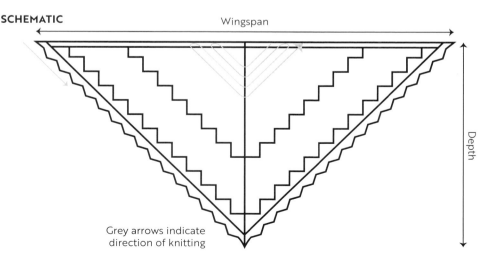

Wingspan

Depth

Grey arrows indicate direction of knitting

Chapter 3

KEY

☐	Knit on RS, purl on WS
•	Knit on WS
⊠	P1 tbl on WS
⊠	K1 tbl on WS
⊙	Yarn over
◿	Ssk on RS
◿	K2tog on RS
◿	K2tog on WS
⊼	K3tog on RS
⊼	Sssk on RS
⊎	SskE on RS
⊻	Sl1 purlwise with yarn in front
◖	Cast off 1 st
■	Stitch remaining on right needle after casting off
☐	Pattern repeat

CHART D KNITTED-ON LACE EDGING

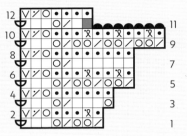

CHART C TULIP TO GARTER TRANSITION

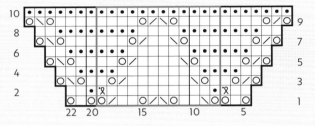

CHART B TULIP LACE PATTERN

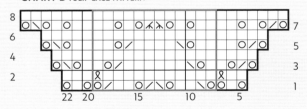

CHART A GARTER TO TULIP TRANSITION

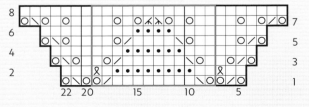

PROJECT **BITHYNICA SHAWL**

PATTERN NOTES

This triangular shawl is worked from the centre back neck outwards. The back neck is cast on using the nifty garter tab cast-on method (see page 52 for photo tutorial). Yarn over increases are then used at the edges and centre to create two large triangles. The first section is worked in garter stitch, before transitioning to a Tulip Lace pattern, and back to garter stitch. A knitted-on lace edging completes the shawl, and features large double yarn over holes.

SPECIAL TECHNIQUES

Photo tutorials for the following techniques can be found within this book.

Garter tab cast-on method (page 52)
Working yarn overs, including at the start of a row (page 7 onwards)
Reading lace charts (page 13)
Working double yarn overs (page 54)
Blocking lace (page 46)

The following video tutorials may be found on our website at **www.acknitwear.co.uk/something-new-to-learn-about-lace**

Garter tab cast-on method
Working yarn overs
Adding a knitted-on edging
Blocking lace

1 GARTER TAB CAST ON

Using waste yarn, a crochet hook and 3.75mm knitting needles, provisionally cast on 3 sts.
Change to main yarn and knit 7 rows.
Turn through 90° and pick up and knit 3 sts along the row-end edge of the tab. Turn through 90° and carefully remove the waste yarn at the cast-on edge and pick up and knit the 3 sts revealed. *9 sts.*

2 GARTER STITCH CENTRE

Row 1 (RS): *K3, pm, yo twice, pm; rep from * once more, k3. *4 sts inc; 13 sts.*
Row 2 (WS): *K3, slm, k1, k1 tbl, slm; rep from * once more, k3.
Row 3: *K3, slm, yo, knit to marker, yo, slm; rep from * once more, k3. *4 sts inc.*
Row 4: Knit to end, slipping markers.
Rep last 2 rows a further 48 times. *196 sts inc; 209 sts.*

Move to step 3 for charted instructions and step 4 for written instructions.

3 TULIP LACE BORDER –
CHARTED INSTRUCTIONS

Row 1 (RS): *K3, slm, reading from right to left, work across row 1 of chart A, repeating the marked section 8 times in total, slm; rep from * once more, k3. *4 sts inc.*
Row 2 (WS): *K3, slm, reading from left to right, work across row 2 of chart A, repeating the marked section 8 times in total, slm; rep from * once more, k3.
Last 2 rows set chart A pattern. Cont to work from chart A as set, increasing as indicated, until chart A row 8 is complete. *20 sts inc; 229 sts.*

Row 9 (RS): *K3, slm, reading from right to left, work across row 1 of chart B, repeating the marked section 9 times in total, slm; rep from * once more, k3. *8 sts inc.*

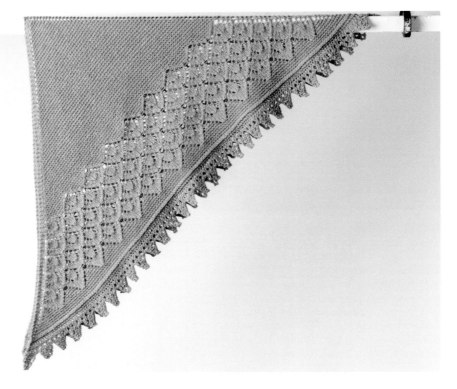

Row 10 (WS): *K3, slm, reading from left to right, work across row 2 of chart B, repeating the marked section 9 times in total, slm; rep from * once more, k3.

Last 2 rows set chart B pattern. Cont to work from chart B as set, increasing as indicated, until chart B row 8 is complete. *24 sts inc; 253 sts.*

Work chart B a second time, now repeating the marked section 10 times on each side of the shawl. *24 sts inc; 277 sts.*

Work chart B a third time, now repeating the marked section 11 times on each side of the shawl. *24 sts inc; 301 sts.*

Work chart B a fourth time, now repeating the marked section 12 times on each side of the shawl. *24 sts inc; 325 sts.*

Row 41 (RS): *K3, slm, reading from right to left, work across row 1 of chart C, repeating the marked section 13 times in total, slm; rep from * once more, k3. *8 sts inc.*

Row 42 (WS): *K3, slm, reading from left to right, work across row 2 of chart C, repeating the marked section 13 times in total, slm; rep from * once more, k3.

Last 2 rows set chart C pattern. Cont to work from chart C as set, increasing as indicated, until chart C row 10 is complete. *24 sts inc; 349 sts.*

Move to step 5.

4 TULIP LACE BORDER –
WRITTEN INSTRUCTIONS

Row 1 (RS): **K3, slm, yo, k2tog, yo, *yo, ssk, k8, k2tog, yo; rep from * to 2 sts before marker, yo, ssk, yo, slm; rep from ** once more, k3. *4 sts inc; 213 sts.*

Row 2 (WS): **K3, slm, p3, *p1 tbl, p1, k8, p2; rep from * to 3 sts before marker, p1 tbl, p2, slm; rep from ** once more, k3.

Row 3: **K3, slm, yo, k2tog, yo, k1, *k1, yo, ssk, k6, k2tog, yo, k1; rep from * to 3 sts before marker, k1, yo, ssk, yo, slm; rep from ** once more, k3. *4 sts inc; 217 sts.*

Row 4: **K3, slm, p4, *p3, k6, p3; rep from * to 4 sts before marker, p4, slm; rep from ** once more, k3.

Row 5: **K3, slm, yo, k2tog, yo, k2, *k2, yo, ssk, k4, k2tog, yo, k2; rep from * to 4 sts before marker, k2, yo, ssk, yo, slm; rep from ** once more, k3. *4 sts inc; 221 sts.*

Row 6: **K3, slm, p5, *p4, k4, p4; rep from * to 5 sts before marker, p5, slm; rep from ** once more, k3.

Row 7: **K3, slm, yo, k2tog, yo, k1, yo, k2, *k2, yo, k1, yo, sssk, k3tog, yo, k1, yo, k2; rep from * to 5 sts before marker, k2, yo, k1, yo, ssk, yo, slm; rep from ** once more, k3. *8 sts inc; 229 sts.*

Row 8: *K3, slm, purl to marker, slm; rep from * once more, k3.

Row 9 (RS): **K3, slm, yo, k1, yo, *yo, ssk, k2, yo, ssk, k2tog, yo, k2, k2tog, yo; rep from * to 1 st before marker, yo, k1, yo, slm; rep from ** once more, k3. *8 sts inc.*

Row 10 (WS): **K3, slm, p3, *p1 tbl, p11; rep from * to 3 sts before marker, p1 tbl, p2, slm; rep from ** once more, k3.

Row 11: **K3, slm, yo, k2tog, yo, k1, *k1, yo, ssk, k6, k2tog, yo, k1; rep from * to 3 sts before marker, k1, yo, ssk, yo, slm; rep from ** once more, k3. *4 sts inc.*

Row 12: *K3, slm, purl to marker, slm; rep from * once more, k3.

Row 13: **K3, slm, yo, k2tog, yo, k2, *k2, yo, ssk, k4, k2tog, yo, k2; rep from * to 4 sts before marker, k2, yo, ssk, yo; rep from ** once more, k3. *4 sts inc.*

Row 14: As row 12.

Row 15: **K3, slm, yo, k2tog, yo, k1, yo, k2, *k2, yo, k1, yo, sssk, k3tog, yo, k1, yo, k2; rep from * to 5 sts before marker, k2, yo, k1, yo, ssk, yo, slm; rep from ** once more, k3. *8 sts inc.*

Row 16: As row 12.

Rows 9–16 set Tulip Lace pattern. Rep rows 9–16 a further 3 times. *96 sts inc; 325 sts.*

Row 41 (RS): As row 9. *8 sts inc; 333 sts.*

Row 42 (WS): **K3, slm, p2, k1, *k1 tbl, p10, k1; rep from * to 3 sts before marker, k1 tbl, p2, slm; rep from ** once more, k3.

Row 43: As row 11. *4 sts inc; 337 sts.*

Row 44: **K3, slm, p2, k2, *k2, p8, k2; rep from * to 4 sts before marker, k2, p2, slm; rep from ** once more, k3.

Row 45: As row 13. *4 sts inc; 341 sts.*

Row 46: **K3, slm, p2, k3, *k3, p6, k3; rep from * to 5 sts before marker, k3, p2, slm; rep from ** once more, k3.

Row 47: **K3, slm, yo, k2tog, yo, k3, *k3, yo, ssk, k2, k2tog, yo, k3; rep from * to 5 sts before marker, k3, yo, ssk, yo, slm; rep from ** once more, k3. *4 sts inc; 345 sts.*

Row 48: **K3, slm, p2, k4, *k4, p4, k4; rep from * to 6 sts before marker, k4, p2, slm; rep from ** once more, k3.

Row 49: **K3, slm, yo, k2tog, yo, k4, *k4, yo, ssk, k2tog, yo, k4; rep from * to 6 sts before marker, k4, yo, ssk, yo, slm; rep from ** once more, k3. *4 sts inc; 349 sts.*

Row 50: Knit to end, slipping markers.

Move to step 5.

5 GARTER STITCH BORDER
Row 1 (RS): *K3, slm, yo, knit to marker, yo, slm; rep from * once more, k3. *4 sts inc.*
Row 2 (WS): Knit to end, slipping markers.
Rep last 2 rows a further 3 times. *16 sts inc; 365 sts.*

Move to step 6 for charted instructions and step 7 for written instructions.

**6 KNITTED-ON LACE EDGING –
CHARTED INSTRUCTIONS**
With RS facing, working yarn and the knitted cast-on method, cast on 7 sts to the left needle tip. *7 edging sts; 365 centre sts.*

Row 1 (RS): Reading from right to left, work across row 1 of chart D. *1 edging st inc; 8 edging sts; 1 centre st dec.*
Row 2 (WS): Reading from left to right, work across row 2 of chart D.
Last 2 rows set chart D pattern. Cont to work from chart D as set, increasing and decreasing as indicated, until chart row 12 is complete for the 30th time. *7 edging sts; 180 centre sts dec; 185 centre sts remain.*

On the 31st repeat of chart D, rows 5 and 7 will both be joined to the same centre st of the shawl as foll:
Work rows 1–4 as normal.
On row 5, when working the sskE join, leave the centre stitch on the left needle tip (instead of slipping it off as you complete the decrease).
Work row 6 as normal.
On row 7, when you work the sskE join, you will be joining the edging st and the centre st that is *also* joined to row 5.
Work rows 8-12 as normal. *7 edging sts; 5 centre sts dec; 180 centre sts remain.*

Rep 12 rows of chart D a further 29 times. *7 edging sts; 174 centre sts dec; 6 centre sts remain.*

Work chart D rows 1–11 once more. *7 edging sts; 6 centre sts dec; 0 centre sts remain.*

Cast off remaining 7 sts knitwise.

Move to step 8.

**7 KNITTED-ON LACE EDGING –
WRITTEN INSTRUCTIONS**
With RS facing, working yarn and the knitted cast-on method, cast on 7 sts to the left needle tip.

Row 1 (RS): K2tog, yo twice, k2tog, yo, k2, sskE. *1 edging st inc; 8 edging sts; 1 centre st dec.*
Row 2 (WS): Sl1 pwise wyif, k2tog, yo, k3, k1 tbl, k1.
Row 3: Yo, k3, k2tog, yo, k2, sskE. *1 edging st inc; 9 edging sts; 1 centre st dec.*
Row 4: Sl1 pwise wyif, k2tog, yo, k6.
Row 5: [K2tog, yo twice] twice, k2tog, yo, k2, sskE. *2 edging sts inc; 11 edging sts; 1 centre st dec.*
Row 6: Sl1 pwise wyif, k2tog, yo, k3, k1 tbl, k2, k1 tbl, k1.
Row 7: K6, k2tog, yo, k2, sskE. *1 centre st dec.*
Row 8: Sl1 pwise wyif, k2tog, yo, k8.
Row 9: [K2tog, yo twice] 3 times, k2tog, yo, k2, sskE. *3 edging sts inc; 14 edging sts; 1 centre st dec.*
Row 10: Sl1 pwise wyif, k2tog, yo, k3, [k1 tbl, k2] twice, k1 tbl, k1.
Row 11: Cast off 7 sts (1 st remains on right needle), k1, k2tog, yo, k2, sskE. *7 edging sts dec; 7 edging sts remain; 1 centre st dec.*
Row 12: Sl1 pwise wyif, k2tog, yo, k4.
Rows 1–12 set Edging Lace pattern. Rep rows 1–12 a further 29 times. *7 edging sts; 180 centre sts dec; 185 centre sts remain.*

On the 31st repeat of rows 1–12, rows 5 and 7 will both be joined to the same centre st of the shawl as foll:
Work rows 1–4 as normal.

On row 5, when working the sskE join, leave the centre stitch on the left needle tip (instead of slipping it off as you complete the decrease).

Work row 6 as normal.

On row 7, when you work the sskE join, you will be joining the edging st and the centre st that is *also* joined to row 5.

Work rows 8-12 as normal. *7 edging sts; 5 centre sts dec; 180 centre sts remain.*

Rep rows 1–12 a further 29 times. *7 edging sts; 174 centre sts dec; 6 centre sts remain.* Rep rows 1–11 once more. *7 edging sts; 6 centre sts dec; 0 centre sts remain.*

Cast off remaining 7 sts knitwise.

Move to step 8.

8 FINISHING

Weave in all ends but do not trim.

Soak your shawl in lukewarm water and wool wash for 20 minutes. Squeeze out excess water (but do not wring). Press between towels to dry further. Lay your shawl flat to dry, threading wires or strong cotton along the straight garter stitch edges and pinning out the peaks of the lace edging. Stretch the fabric firmly in all directions to open up the lace patterns. Measure both sides of the top edge, to ensure that they are even. Check that the centre spine is perpendicular to the top edge with a set square, or by checking that both halves of the lace edging are the same length. When the shawl is completely dry, trim any remaining ends.

SOMETHING NEW TO LEARN ABOUT **LACE**

YARN

We are thrilled to launch our first yarn, **Something to Knit With 4ply**, which we have had spun especially for this book about lace. The blend of fibres combines the properties of highland wool and alpaca to give a yarn that is both springy and soft. The fabric made from this yarn is great at a range of tensions, whether larger needles are used to give it drape in a shawl, or smaller needles are used to give a slightly firmer, warmer fabric. It doesn't split easily, even when working with the sharpest of needles, and holds the stitches well, so that if you happen to drop them from your needles, you will be able to pick them up easily. We have chosen a colour range that will allow your lace to shine, with solid colours ensuring that every stitch allows the patterning to take centre stage. **Something to Knit With 4ply** is available from the following retailers:

UK: *shop.acknitwear.co.uk*
Germany: *www.strickmich.shop*
USA: *www.masondixonknitting.com*

OTHER EQUIPMENT

Stitch markers, blocking wires and mats, interchangeable circular needles, and other equipment for getting the most out of your lace are all available from our shop:

shop.acknitwear.co.uk

Blocking frames (as seen on page 51) are available from Obscure Designs on Etsy:

www.etsy.com/uk/shop/ObscureDesignsPH

TENSION

Tension (US gauge) information is given for each project. If you don't match tension with the recommended needle size, try again with smaller or larger needles as required. Yarn quantity used and finished size are determined by matching tension correctly. All yarn quantities include 5% for swatching.

WHERE TO FIND US?

You can follow Jen and Jim on...

RAVELRY	JenACKnitwear
	VeufTricot
FACEBOOK	Arnall-Culliford Knitwear
INSTAGRAM	@jenacknitwear
	@veuftricot
TWITTER	@jenacknitwear
	@veuftricot
YOUTUBE	JenACKnitwear
OUR BLOG	www.acknitwear.co.uk/blog

Visit **shop.acknitwear.co.uk** to see our full range of books, yarns and other knitting accessories.

SUPPORT

If you require help with any of the techniques, or patterns, do join us in our friendly group on Ravelry at Arnall-Culliford Knitwear:

www.ravelry.com/groups/arnall-culliford-knitwear

You may find your question has already been asked, and if not, there are lots of helpful and friendly knitters around to assist you. Your question may also help others, so please don't hesitate to post to our group.

DOWNLOAD

For technical assistance with your purchase of *Something New to Learn About Lace,* please email **jim@acknitwear.co.uk**.

VIDEO TUTORIALS

We have created video tutorials to accompany *Something New to Learn About Lace*, and they can all be found on our website at:

www.acknitwear.co.uk/something-new-to-learn-about-lace

You will also find a selection of general video tutorials on our website:

www.acknitwear.co.uk/tutorials-1

Information

THE TEAM

JEN ARNALL-CULLIFORD
Technical editor, teacher, designer, and holder of three Blue Peter badges, Jen brings knitting to the knitters. She draws on a huge wealth of knowledge and experience, and her eye for detail to write the tutorials as well as to design for this book.

JIM ARNALL-CULLIFORD
Formerly a science teacher, Jim still wields a red pen with aplomb, editing patterns and checking over the knitting content from a learner's point of view. In working on this project, Jim's steep knitting learning curve has continued as he tested out the tutorials in producing many of the swatches featured.

NIC BLACKMORE **Art and Production Editor**
Without Nic, there would be no book. She magically amalgamates the mess of files and photographs we chuck at her to produce the clean design and layouts. She and Jen would get a lot more done if they stayed off Skype, but their lives would be infinitely more dull in consequence.

JESSE WILD **Photographer**
As well as shooting pro cyclists and rock legends, Jesse is an expert knitwear photographer. He has an eye for ensuring that every stitch can be seen clearly to produce images of the highest quality. He can also be trusted to keep the mood light so that every photoshoot is as relaxed as possible. *www.jessewild.co.uk*

SALLY SOMERS **Chief Knit-picker**
Sally brings her remarkable intelligence to scrutinise the nation's cookery books so that they make sense and work. We are incredibly lucky that she has turned her hand to knitting and has been able to cast her eye over this book to eliminate inconsistency and ambiguity.

MARTINA BEHM **Designer**
If you ever flick through Ravelry's *Hot Right Now* pages, you are sure to come across Martina's patterns. She takes fairly simple techniques and produces complex-looking projects. Her designs are the best of all worlds: interesting and moreish to knit, easy enough to work on in company, and they leave you with an eminently wearable item. *www.strickmich.frischetexte.de/en*

DONNA SMITH **Designer**
As Shetland Wool Week Patron in 2015, Donna designed the iconic Baa-ble Hat, and has continued to produce beautiful, wearable designs. Donna takes inspiration from the stunning surroundings of her home in Shetland. Steeped in textile culture and history, Donna is passionate about passing on the traditional knitting techniques of Shetland. *www.donnasmithdesigns.co.uk*

Information

ACKNOWLEDGEMENTS

When we first decided we would like to develop our own yarn range, there was never any doubt in our minds about who we would approach to help us to realise our plans: Jeni Hewlett and Andy Robinson of Chester Wool Company have been supportive and encouraging at every step, helping us to fulfil our yarny dreams. Thank you both!

We are lucky to have incredibly supportive friends in Frome, in particular Pepita Collins for allowing us the run of her beautiful house for the photo shoot, Sue McGovern for once again agreeing to model, and Tina and Edie for being game first-time models. We are thrilled with the photos!

I am unutterably grateful to Julie Dexter and Jim for their help with knitting the lace swatches for the tutorials. My knitting time is in such short supply that the book wouldn't have been possible without them. Thanks are also due to Kim Hobley for kindly knitting the beautiful Aphaca baby blanket.

Our Ravelry group is full of enthusiasm and knitting wisdom, for which we are most thankful, and in particular to Alix, Katherine, Maylin and Nancy for being so generous with their precious time in supporting us as moderators.

The last three months have been extraordinarily busy, and without the support of our parents, we would have hit the buffers long ago. Thank you all.

**ALSO AVAILABLE FROM
ARNALL-CULLIFORD KNITWEAR:**

Information

cdd   centred double decrease; slip next 2 stitches together (as if to knit 2 together), knit 1, then pass both slipped stitches over (2 stitches decreased)

cont   continue(d)/continues/continuing

dec   decrease(d)/decreases/decreasing

foll   follow(s)/following

inc   increase(d)/increases/increasing

k   knit

k2tog   knit next 2 stitches together (1 stitch decreased)

k3tog   knit next 3 stitches together (2 stitches decreased)

kfb   knit into front and back of next stitch (1 stitch increased)

kwise   knitwise

M1   make 1 stitch by lifting the bar between stitches from front to back and knitting into the back of this loop (1 stitch increased)

p   purl

pm   place marker

psso   pass slipped stitch over

pwise   purlwise

rep   repeat(s)/repeating

RS   right side

s2sk   slip next 2 stitches as if to k2tog, slip next stitch knitwise, insert left needle into the front of all 3 slipped stitches and knit them together (2 stitches decreased)

sl   slip stitch(es) purlwise, unless otherwise stated

slm   slip marker

ssk   slip 1 stitch knitwise, slip 1 stitch purlwise (or knitwise), return both stitches to left needle without twisting and knit them together through the back loop (1 stitch decreased)

sskE   work as ssk, the first slipped stitch comes from the edging, and the second slipped stitch is a centre stitch, thus joining the edging to the centre of the shawl (1 centre stitch decreased)

sssk   slip 3 stitches separately, knitwise, return all 3 stitches to left needle without twisting and knit them together through the back loop (2 stitches decreased)

st(s)   stitch(es)

w&t   wrap & turn; with yarn at back, slip next stitch purlwise from left to right needle, bring yarn to front between the needle tips, return slipped stitch to left needle, turn ready to work the next row leaving all remaining stitches unworked

WS   wrong side

wyib   with yarn in back

wyif   with yarn in front